JARROLD SHORT WALKS

for all the family

the
Cotswolds

Compiled by
John Brooks

Mapping sourced from Ordnance Survey®

D0812906

Acknowledgements

The publishers are grateful to the National Trust for allowing inclusion of walks at Woodchester and Sherborne Park. David Armstrong, Warden at Woodchester, kindly checked the text and provided additional information.

Text: John Brooks
Photography: John Brooks
Editor: Geoffrey Sutton
Designer: Doug Whitworth

© Jarrold Publishing 2001

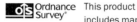 **Ordnance Survey®** This product includes mapping data licensed from Ordnance Survey ® with the permission of the Controller of Her Majesty's Stationery Office. © Crown Copyright 2001. All rights reserved. Licence number 100017593. Pathfinder is a registered trade mark of Ordnance Survey, the national mapping agency of Great Britain.

Jarrold Publishing ISBN 0-7117-1602-1

First published 2001
by Jarrold Publishing

Printed in Belgium
by Proost NV, Turnhout. 1/01

Jarrold Publishing
Pathfinder Guides, Whitefriars,
Norwich NR3 1TR
E-mail: pathfinder@jarrold.com
www.jarroldpublishing.co.uk/
pathfinders

Front cover: Snowshill
Previous page: Blockley

Contents

Keymap   4

Introduction   6

Walks

Short, easy walks

1 *Sherborne Park*   10
2 *Cirencester Town and Park*   13
3 *Eastleach Turville and Eastleach Martin*   16
4 *Misarden Park*   19
5 *Chedworth*   22
6 *Cleeve Hill*   25
7 *Leckhampton Hill*   28
8 *Sezincote from Bourton-on-the-Hill*   31

Walks of modest length, likely to involve some modest uphill walking

9   *Chastleton from Adlestrop*   34
10 *Haresfield Beacon*   37
11 *Minchinhampton Common*   40
12 *Snowshill*   43
13 *Batsford from Blockley*   46
14 *Lost village of Widford from Burford*   50
15 *Farmington from Northleach*   54
16 *Woodchester Park*   58

More challenging walks which may be longer and/or over
more rugged terrain, often with some stiff climbs

17 *The Slaughters from Bourton-on-the-Water*   61
18 *Winchcombe and Hailes Abbey*   65
19 *Guiting Wood*   69
20 *Bibury and Coln St Aldwyns*   72

Further Information   76
Walking Safety; Follow the Country Code;
The Cotswold Voluntary Warden Service;
Useful Organisations; Ordnance Survey Maps
Answers to Questions   79

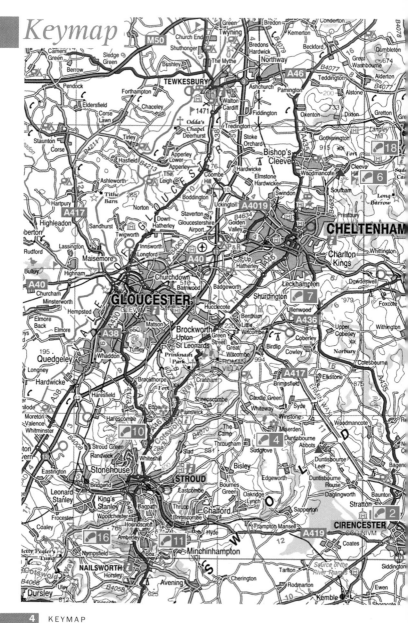

Keymap

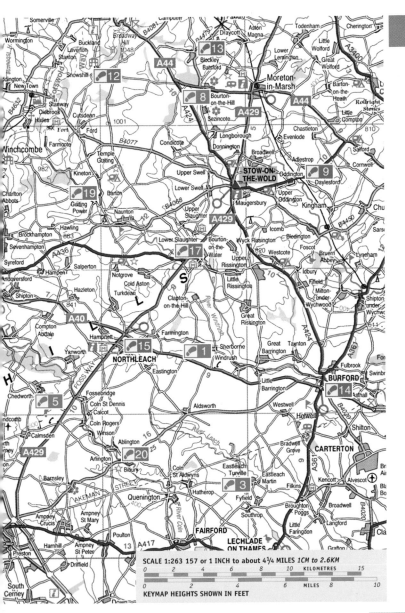

SCALE 1:263 157 or 1 INCH to about 4¼ MILES *1CM to 2.6KM*

KILOMETRES

MILES

KEYMAP HEIGHTS SHOWN IN FEET

Introduction

The routes and information in this book have been devised specifically with families and children in mind. All the walks include points of interest as well as a question to provide an objective.

If you, or your children, have not walked before, choose from the shorter walks for your first outings. The purpose is not simply to get from A to B but to enjoy an exploration, which may be just a steady stroll in the countryside.

The walks are graded by length and difficulty, but few landscapes are truly flat, so even shorter walks may involve some ascent. Details are given under Route Features in the first information box for each route. But the precise nature of the ground underfoot will depend on recent weather conditions. If you do set out on a walk and discover the going is harder than you expected, or the weather has deteriorated, do not be afraid to turn back. The route will always be there another day, when you are fitter or the children are more experienced or the weather is better.

Bear in mind that the countryside also changes. Landmarks may disappear, gates may become stiles, rights of way may be altered. However, with the aid of this book and its maps you should be able enjoy many interesting family walks in the countryside.

The Cotswolds

The name 'Cotswold' has a cosy ring to it, evoking images of cottages, green fields and rolling hills. It derives from Saxon words that, together, give the meaning of wooded hollows hidden amidst gentle hills, as true a description of the district today as when it was first coined, some 1,200 years ago.

The landscape and its buildings owe everything to the underlying bedrock, the honey-coloured oolitic limestone that is the hallmark of the Cotswolds and was used not only for unpretentious churches and cottages, but also for Oxford colleges and the elegant façades of

Georgian Bath and Regency Cheltenham.

The area covers a considerable area of midland and southern England extending from near Stratford-upon-Avon in the north to Wotton-under-Edge, on the doorstep of Bath, to the south. A steep escarpment runs south-west along this line, giving wonderful views over the plain of the River Severn to the uplands of east Wales, while to the east the land dips more gradually to the Thames Valley.

Bourton-on-the-Hill

Early History and the Landscape

Prehistoric settlers were probably attracted to the Cotswolds by the ease with which they could walk over the rolling limestone hills. The main evidence of their occupation is seen in the long barrows where they buried their dead, the most famous being those of Belas Knap near Winchcombe and Hetty Pegler's Tump at Uley.

During the Bronze Age, new settlers began building hillforts, another feature of the upland landscape in the Cotswolds. Their presence speaks of further invasions, when villages would take all their livestock and possessions behind the defences – earthen ramparts encircling a timber stockade – in the hope that they would be able to resist a siege.

The Romans found these defences easy to overcome and subsequently set up military headquarters in Gloucester and Cirencester. The villas at Chedworth and Witcombe are both large and luxurious and their owners must have had all of the amenities enjoyed at home.

Amongst the animals the Romans introduced were sheep with exceptionally long fleeces, and cloth from these was exported throughout the empire. Many centuries after Roman occupation, these animals – known as Cotswold Lions – brought a new prosperity to the region. At the end of the 12th century wool was being exported to weavers in Flanders and arable land, cultivated by ridge and furrow methods, was left unploughed to create sheep-walks. This, with the Black Death, brought about rural depopulation, and many villages were abandoned.

It was soon discovered that Cotswold weavers could also produce cloth of high quality. By the end of the 14th century hardly any wool was exported. Instead, vast quantities of cloth were sent to the quays at Bristol and the wool merchants of the wolds and the weavers who made the cloth in the towns were amongst the wealthiest men in the kingdom.

The Cotswolds enjoyed many natural advantages in cloth-making. The streams flowing through its valleys were reliable and the climate damp, the latter vital if the wool was to have fine texture. Teasels to raise the nap of the cloth and woad to dye it grew in abundance in the clay soil of the Severn vale and there were also deposits of fuller's earth (important for cleaning and shrinking the finished product) near three of the principal cloth-producing towns – Minchinhampton, Stroud and Dursley.

Effigy of Sir Lawrence Tunfield, Lord Chief Baron of the Exchequer under James I, in Burford church

The medieval wool magnates were not slow in spending the rewards they won from their trade.

Most obviously, they gave their thanks to God and sought paths to redemption by endowing abbeys and building or enlarging churches.

The merchants also built fine houses for themselves while the craftspeople they employed were content with more humble homes in the towns and villages where they worked. Many of their cottages, some dating from the 15th and 16th centuries, survive and give the Cotswolds their unique character.

From Tudor to Modern Times

Cloth-making continued to be an important part of the region's economy until the end of the 19th century with the industry mainly centred on Stroud and neighbouring towns. The greatest change to the landscape and economy in early Tudor times was caused by the abolition of the monasteries. Some adapted monastic buildings into mansions for themselves, others built grand houses for themselves away from the religious foundations. The king had unwittingly introduced a new class into society – the landed gentry – who would play an increasingly important role in the development of the Cotswold countryside.

The infamous Inclosure Acts gave landlords the right to enclose common land. Previously the commons had been where village dwellers had the right to graze their livestock, gather firewood and cultivate small plots. When these privileges were withdrawn, cottagers were often unable to pay rent and were evicted. From about 1670 until the mid-19th century there was a steady exodus from the countryside. This continued as machinery was introduced to agriculture, and the process continues today as ever-larger tractors reduce the need for farmhands.

The Cotswolds have an array of stately homes from all periods. Most of them are surrounded by areas of parkland laid out when the houses were built, and walking through them is a delight.

All that remains is to wish the reader happy walking. May the weather be fair and the going good – whatever the season there is always fresh beauty to be found in the countryside of the Cotswolds, and there is no better way of seeing it than on foot.

1 *Sherborne Park*

START National Trust's Ewepen car park, Sherborne

DISTANCE 2½ miles (4km)

TIME 2 hours

PARKING At start – small charge to non-members of National Trust

ROUTE FEATURES A parkland and woodland walk, easy going

The National Trust have done excellent work in opening parts of the Sherborne Park estate to the public. The well-maintained paths lead to many interesting features and each season brings fresh beauty to the eyes of the visitor. The 4,140-acre (1,675 ha) estate came to the National Trust on the death of Lord Sherborne in 1982. Sherborne House and stables, divided into luxury flats, are not open to the public.

Ewepen Barn, the starting point, was built around 1860, and the surrounding yard was used to shelter sheep in winter, as the name suggests. Almost certainly the barn was also used for winnowing grain after harvest as the main door faces the prevailing wind from the south-west. The barn now serves the National Trust as an information centre.

Where did the ice for an ice-house come from?

Turn right out of the car park and take the right fork to follow the green route in an anticlockwise direction. Pass the cricket and rugby field to come to a point where the drive from the Cheltenham Lodges crosses the track **A**. A beech avenue, magnificent in autumn, leads up to the lodge gates on the A40.

Continue ahead on the track – this point is almost 600ft (183m) above sea-level and gives wonderful views northwards. Where a notice tells you that 'the driveway becomes

PUBLIC TRANSPORT None

REFRESHMENTS None

PUBLIC TOILETS None

ORDNANCE SURVEY MAPS Outdoor Leisure 45 (The Cotswolds)

private beyond this point' **B**, turn left through an iron gate.

The path follows the right-hand edge of Quarry Wood. The quarry, now screened by trees, supplied stone for St Paul's Cathedral and many of the Oxford colleges. Note that a few elms are becoming re-established here amongst the yews, beeches and oaks.

Snowdrops in Sherborne Park

Larger than it looks from the outside, it was built in a shady place and extends underground.

Beyond an iron gate there is a beautiful grassy area surrounding a circular seat made around a yew tree. This is the Pleasure Ground made as a shrubbery where paths wind over miniature hills planted with snowdrops and other bulbs. The path descends to pass a pair of

The path leaves the wood to pass the ice-house, which probably dates from the early 19th century.

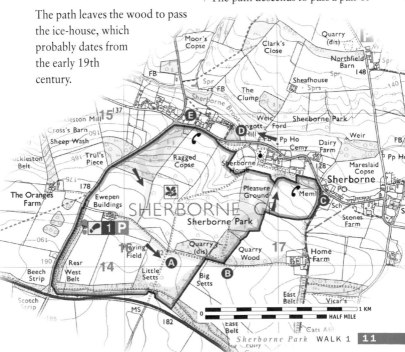

massive firs and then swings right after a glimpse of Sherborne House.

When you come to the edge of the wood again, by ancient beech trees, go left to follow railings past a magnificent yew. It was probably growing here when the Duttons came to Sherborne in 1551. Daffodils bloom here, preceded by a display of aconites, and there is a good view of the house and gardens.

The path emerges from the park into the village by the war memorial **C**. Turn left – there is a view of the lovely Sherborne Brook to the right, which has been widened into lakes flowing over cascades. To the left is the stable block, itself a minor stately home. A path to the church leads up from the end of the stables.

To see the oldest cottages in Sherborne

The **Sherborne estate** originally belonged to Winchcombe Abbey and was bought by Thomas Dutton in 1551 when the abbey was 'dissolved'. Traces of Dutton's house survive in the present building which largely dates from 1829 to 1834 when it was rebuilt for the 2nd Lord Sherborne. The mansion and stables are private, now converted into luxury apartments. The church was rebuilt at the same time as the house, possibly to designs by Anthony Salvin.

take the path on the right through a green gate **D**. These are at the western end of the village. The eastern end, beyond the war memorial, was rebuilt as a model village in the mid-19th century.

A lane leads back to the main street. Turn right for a few yards before going left through a gap in the wall **E**. When the path divides go left to climb away from the road and the wall to the top corner of the wood. The path follows iron railings back to Ewepen Barn.

The ice-house

Cirencester Town and Park

Not only is Cirencester the most historic of Cotswold market towns, it can also claim to be the most beautiful with an out- standing church and town houses dating from the 15th century onwards. There is also the extensive park on the west side of the town where people can enjoy the classic view of church and town from Broad Ride.

START Cirencester church
DISTANCE 2½ miles (4km)
TIME 1½ hours
PARKING Waterloo long-stay car park (walk to church from north end of car park by flats, following river at first, then crossing it and turning left through Abbey Gardens)
ROUTE FEATURES A level walk through the market town, dating from Roman times, and a beautiful park (open 08.00–17.00)

2

From the church tower, turn right along Dollar Street. Note No. 2, bearing the first of several blue civic plaques you will see. This one informs that the abbey mill once stood here. A little further on Dollar Street House was built for a lawyer, Joseph Pitt, who sponsored Pittsville Spa in Cheltenham early in the 19th century.

> **?** *Where did the money to build the tower of St John the Baptist Church come from?*

Keep ahead into Gloucester Street to pass the White Lion inn.

Broad Ride, Cirencester Park

PUBLIC TRANSPORT Tel. 01452 425543
REFRESHMENTS Pubs and tearooms in Cirencester
PUBLIC TOILETS At Forum, Corinium and Brewery Arts (Tesco) car parks
ORDNANCE SURVEY MAPS Outdoor Leisure 45 (The Cotswolds)

The vanilla-coloured house on the left dates from the 15th century.

Turn left into Barton Lane before the Nelson inn . The battlements seen beyond the playing-fields on the left belong to the Old Barracks on Cecily Hill, built in 1857. Continue down the lane to cross a bridge and enter Cirencester Park. Note that the park is closed to visitors at 17.00.

Turn right at a T-junction in front of a fine barn and follow the road past a grand house. At the end of a high wall to the left there is a crossways. Bear right and climb a short hill to

Three Roman roads meet at Cirencester – Ermine Street, the Fosse Way and Akeman Street – and their town, Corinium Dubunnorum, grew out of an army outpost to become prosperous, second only to London in size and influence. The **Corinium Museum** is the place to learn about Roman life here in the 2nd century AD, with a reconstruction of a mosaics workshop and a host of artefacts on display.

an abandoned farm building. Turn left opposite it and then fork right when the track divides on to North Terrace, which heads westwards with woodland to the left, and to open countryside on the right.

After ½ mile (800m) follow the track to the left past two 'No dogs' notices (which don't seem to apply to these few yards of muddy track) and turn left down Broad Drive.

The vista of church and town at the end of the

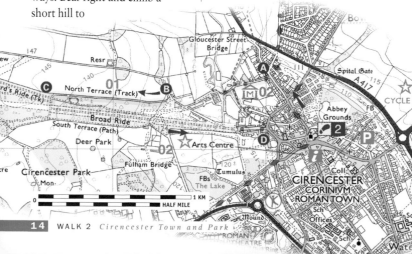

Gazebo in Cirencester Park

drive becomes ever more impressive as you approach the park gates. These give on to Cecily Hill with its romantic array of houses, all different but all built of Cotswold stone.

Turn right into Park Street **D** and at the next junction turn left to pass the Corinium Museum – but pause to look back at the 40ft-(12m) high yew hedge planted in 1720 which, with a stone wall, separates Lord Bathurst's mansion from the town. It is one of the highest yew hedges in the world.

Fork left down Black Jack Street to pass a succession of inviting shops and reach the church. Climb the church tower for a view of Cirencester Park. The house was built between 1714 and 1718 for Lord Bathurst, friend and sponsor of the poet Alexander Pope. The tower also gives a spectacular view of the streets and parkland covered in the walk. ●

St John the Baptist Church is one of the largest parish churches in England and the earliest work dates from the mid-13th century (though a Norman church was here previously and replaced a large Saxon church). Its numerous chapels were built by wool merchants seeking redemption for earthly sins. The enormous south porch – once used as a town hall and as high as the roof of the church – was added in 1490. There is also outstanding medieval glass and the famous Boleyn Cup, made for Anne Boleyn's family and given to the church in 1561.

3 Eastleach Turville and Eastleach Martin

START Eastleach Turville (village noticeboard opposite almshouses)

DISTANCE 2½ miles (4km)

TIME 2 hours

PARKING On-road parking in village. Patrons of the Victoria inn are welcome to use pub car park

ROUTE FEATURES Village, lane and riverside walking; mud possible at point **C**; dogs should be kept on the lead

Until 1935 Eastleach was officially two separate villages with the River Leach running between them. The river gives the place its character, as do the churches standing on each bank. Upstream from Eastleach it is particularly beautiful (though apt to overflow in winter).

From the centre of Eastleach Turville walk down the road and cross the river by the stone footbridge. Daffodils line the bank and provide a foreground for pictures of St Andrew's Church. The footpath goes through the other churchyard, where the 12th-century Church of St Michael and St Martin is in the care of the Churches Conservation Trust. Its interior preserves relics of an earlier age, like oil lamps and ancient benches.

? *Where is the clock tower in Eastleach?*

Turn left out of the church gate and then right on to the lane to Holwell **A**. Follow this for nearly a mile (1.6km) with the River Leach to the left.

Turn off the lane to the left just as it begins to climb **B**, going through a gate bearing a Hatherop estate notice (Dogs to be on leads). The lovely riverside footpath follows the side of the valley where you may well find a heron fishing, or even a kingfisher.

Pass stepping-stones that take a path across the river and could be part of a short cut (though, if the

PUBLIC TRANSPORT None

REFRESHMENTS Pub in Eastleach Turville

PUBLIC TOILETS None

ORDNANCE SURVEY MAPS Outdoor Leisure 45 (The Cotswolds)

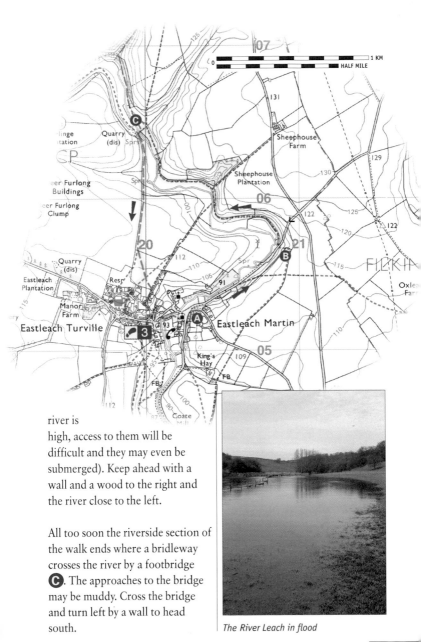

river is
high, access to them will be
difficult and they may even be
submerged). Keep ahead with a
wall and a wood to the right and
the river close to the left.

All too soon the riverside section of
the walk ends where a bridleway
crosses the river by a footbridge
C. The approaches to the bridge
may be muddy. Cross the bridge
and turn left by a wall to head
south.

The River Leach in flood

This is lovely walking with views of the river below. After ½ mile (800m) there is the first in a succession of steel gates and the river is hidden. Continue to walk with the wall close to the right.

When the buildings of Eastleach Turville can be seen ahead, beyond a final meadow, keep ahead to a steel gate by a children's playground. Turn right at a lane and then immediately left down a footpath heading for the tower that embellishes a group of estate cottages. The footpath reaches the

The Keble family settled in Eastleach Turville in Tudor times and its most famous member, **John Keble** (1792–1866), served both churches as curate when he was a young priest. Later he became Professor of Poetry at Oxford and was a founder of the Oxford Movement, which believed that the Church of England should be an evangelical institution rather than a political one. Keble College at Oxford was founded by his supporters as a memorial.

car park of the Victoria inn. Descend to the road below the pub and turn left back to the village centre and the starting point. ●

The River Leach at Eastleach

Misarden Park

START Miserden village centre

DISTANCE 2½ miles (4km). *Shorter version* 1½ miles (2.4km)

TIME 2 hours (1 hour for shorter route)

PARKING On-street parking in village

ROUTE FEATURES Some short, steep stretches, which may be slippery and muddy, those of the shorter walk mostly on secure surfaces

4

The parkland trees and wonderful lake are highlights of both routes (the shorter one follows a woodland trail made by the estate and a leaflet giving information about trees and wildlife is available from the gardens and estate office). The longer route is on rights-of-way that follow woodland paths and tracks as well as a stretch of quiet lane.

From the centre of the village (where a large tree supports an octagonal shelter) turn your back to the Carpenters' Arms and walk downhill to pass the estate office and nursery. Go through the kissing-gate into the park and after 200 yds (183m) along the drive **A** look to the right to see footpath badges on a paling surrounding a sapling. They point the way to a path across the grass that goes to a stone stile leading into a wood. Continue on a path through a wood that soon reaches an intersection of two drives. Cross a stream here to reach the further of the drives and follow the stream down to a bridge spanning the River Frome **B**.

At this point, those wishing to do the shorter version of the walk can, after crossing the bridge, follow the green waymark and turn right off the drive to follow the little river. The slopes to the right beyond the stream are the earthworks of a

> **?** *Can you detect what type of animal has been climbing over the stone stile leading into the wood in the first paragraph?*

PUBLIC TRANSPORT Tel. 01452 425543

REFRESHMENTS Pub at Miserden

PUBLIC TOILETS None

ORDNANCE SURVEY MAPS Explorer 179 (Gloucester, Cheltenham & Stroud), Landranger 163 (Cheltenham & Cirencester)

Norman motte-and-bailey castle. The path goes beneath some magnificent Douglas firs that were planted in Victorian times. The path crosses a small stream before coming to a woodland track. Bear right on to this (it will be muddy after wet weather) and follow it along the edge of the wood to Misarden Park Lake, a beautiful stretch of water in a perfect setting that was created in the 18th century. Kingfishers are regular visitors as well as heron and several varieties of waterfowl.

Cross the bridge over the outfall with care and turn right on to the drive to walk on the other side of the lake. The climb towards the house is steep at times but the views are magnificent, and there are many

rare trees to admire, some newly planted. Turn left to follow the Woodland Trail waymark at a T-junction. An unusual avenue of western red cedars leads up to the house. Turn off this to the right almost at the end, before a wall, climbing a stile into a meadow. Follow the top wall to find a wall stile (steps up the wall) just to the right of the corner. Walk fairly close to the wall at the top to return to the entrance to the park and the village centre.

To continue on the main route, climb up the hill beyond the bridge for ¼ mile (400m) and, where the drive swings sharply right **C**, look

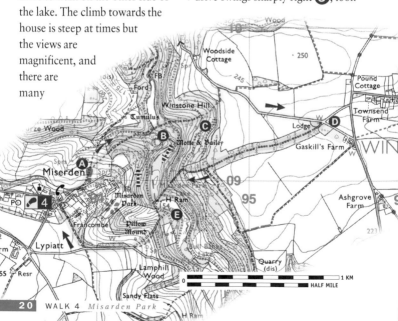

for faint yellow waymarks on the trees. Cross a small causeway to the left by a tiny pond and follow the stencilled yellow arrows uphill through the trees. This is a short but steep climb that leads to a stone stile at the top.

The lake in winter

Turn left to reach a quiet lane and walk along it for about ½ mile (800m) to a gate lodge **D**. Follow the bridleway sign here to go down a grand driveway, but leave it ahead when it swings right towards gateposts topped by stone eagles.

There is a fine view of the mansion as the way continues down past pine trees and crosses another track by pheasant pens. The steep descent may be muddy and slippery but soon a waterfall will be heard and the lake is revealed as you pass a magnificent beech. Cross the outfall from the lake and turn left on to the drive.

Climb for about 75 yds (69m) and, where the drive levels **E**, turn right to follow a footpath sign on to a grassy track that climbs to a kissing-gate. After this go a few steps to the right for a fine view of the lake in its nest of wooded hills.

Continue upwards by following a sunken track through a pasture to another kissing-gate. This gives on to a lane. Walk down this for 300 yds (274m) and where it swings left take the footpath on the right between a fence and a stone wall. Pass the nursery to the right to come out at the village centre by the former school. ●

Misarden Park is the mansion built in 1620 by Sir William Sandys but badly damaged by fire in 1919. Edwin Lutyens was engaged to rebuild the house and he also influenced the layout of the gardens. The outstanding gardens were begun in the 1930s, with their two great herbaceous borders, rose garden, and silver and blue borders. The gardens have continued to develop over the years as has tree-planting in the park. Specimen trees such as Douglas firs reach 100ft (30m) and there are many other interesting varieties that are rare in Britain. Open April–September Tuesday–Thursday.

5 *Chedworth*

START Seven Tuns inn, Chedworth

DISTANCE 2½ miles (4km)

TIME 2 hours

PARKING Seven Tuns car park – alternatively you may prefer to start from the Roman villa and use the woodland walks car park there (closed in winter)

ROUTE FEATURES Paths are steep in places and will be muddy in winter

Chedworth is one of the more remote Cotswold villages. Its cottages are strung along a deep, wooded valley. The famous Roman villa was built in the neighbouring valley, and visitors can see its mosaics, two bathhouses and fascinating artefacts displayed in a museum.

🖊 Take the footpath that climbs from the road opposite the Seven Tuns to the church. The pub dates from 1610 while the airy church lit by Perpendicular windows has a Norman tower. Turn right along the road. Keep ahead when the road swings right, following a sign to the Roman villa.

Cross a stile at the end of the cul-de-sac Ⓐ and bear slightly left to follow the bottom fence. The track

of the railway line that once connected Chedworth with Cheltenham and Cirencester lies on the other side.

Roman mosaic at the villa

> **❓ What type of deity was the shrine in the Roman villa dedicated to?**

PUBLIC TRANSPORT Tel. 01452 425543

REFRESHMENTS Seven Tuns inn

PUBLIC TOILETS At Roman villa

ORDNANCE SURVEY MAPS Outdoor Leisure 45 (The Cotswolds)

Bear left towards the end of the long meadow to climb to a stile into woodland located about 50 yds (46m) from the corner. A flight of steps takes the path to the top of a steep bank. Keep ahead across a bridleway.

The path now follows a field edge and then crosses arable land towards Chedworth Woods. The descent into the woods may be slippery after wet weather, but after this the way is clear on level ground for a short distance before another steep descent to a crossways **B**.

Turn right and continue to descend, going beneath the old railway line. A path on the right leads into the Gloucestershire Wildlife Trust's nature reserve and the one ahead goes to the Roman Villa.

The walk continues by walking down the driveway from the villa, lined by impressive yew trees. Turn

Chedworth saw **military activity** during the Civil War when troops were billeted at the Seven Tuns. The pub also has a memento of the Second World War – a window from one of the huts used to house Italian prisoners working at the airfield. The latter was a Fighter Command base operational from 1942. Ammunition trains used to shelter from attack in the railway tunnel beneath the village! From June 1944 the United States Air Force used the airfield.

right **C** on to a bridleway just beyond the entrance to the National Trust's woodland car park (closed in winter). When the track divides, fork left and begin to climb. After about ½ mile (800m) join a farm track at the top to reach a fiveways **D**.

Keep ahead to follow the Monarch's Way sign to pass a cattle yard and reach a road. Turn right and at the first bend go left on to an enclosed

Chedworth Roman Villa was one of the largest villas in England, and more than a mile (1.6km) of its walls can still be traced. Visitors to the villa will see fine mosaics, a shrine to a deity, the central heating system, two bath-houses and even the latrine. A museum has a display of objects found on the site, which is in the care of the National Trust; tel. 01242 890256 for times of opening.

footpath that descends to Chedworth. Keep ahead when it divides before a gate and a broken stile.

Cross a road by a row of cottages and go down to a stream crossed by a stone bridge. After a stone stile the path climbs to a wooden one that takes it across the old railway embankment. Turn right after another stile to follow the top of a field and then walk past stables to a road back by the Seven Tuns. ●

St Andrew's Church, Chedworth

Cleeve Hill

START Cleeve Hill, golf clubhouse

DISTANCE 3¼ miles (5.2km)

TIME 2½ hours

PARKING Park in disused quarry just beyond clubhouse; alternative car park at point **A**

ROUTE FEATURES Good walking mainly on springy turf with very little climbing, starting close to the top of the hill and following contours. Do not attempt the route in mist and watch out for golfers

Cheltenham owes its origins to mineral-rich springs whose properties were supposed to cure a wide variety of ailments. In tandem with this natural asset its situation, sheltered by high ground to the north and east, must also have been beneficial to health. The climb to the summit of Cleeve Hill from the town centre would be arduous and time-consuming whereas the walk described here involves little climbing.

Turn left from the quarry car park and walk in front of the clubhouse along the lower edge of Cleeve Common. The track drops down close to the road **A**, where there are public toilets.

The summit of **Cleeve Hill** is the highest point in the Cotswolds at 1,083ft (330m) above sea-level. Its position on the edge of the steep escarpment overlooking the Vale of Severn makes it a wonderful viewpoint and keen eyes will identify Gloucester, Tewkesbury, the Malverns and Bredon Hill.

Continue along the eastern edge of Cleeve Common to pass a hotel car park overlooked by a castellated tower and come to a crossways by a cattle-grid. Bear slightly left on to the upper of two lanes to follow a 'Public Path' sign and pass behind Laburnum Cottage and Cheesecake Well (another cottage). The Ring –

> ***?*** *Famous sportsmen used to train on Cleeve Common, one of whom is said to haunt Prestbury, just below the hill. Can you work out which sport?*

PUBLIC TRANSPORT Tel. 01452 425543

REFRESHMENTS Golf club welcomes visitors for lunches and light refreshments

PUBLIC TOILETS By main road near point **A**

ORDNANCE SURVEY MAPS Explorer 179 (Gloucester, Cheltenham & Stroud), Landranger 163 (Cheltenham & Cirencester)

an Iron Age fort – can be seen to the left.

Take the track (asphalted at first) that climbs to the corner of Thrift Wood. The fine beech trees here are glorious in autumn. At the end of the wood leave the track to the left **B** on a path blocked to vehicles by two large boulders. This takes you to the left of the huddle of houses at

> Although it may seem that you are walking just on grass, look carefully and you will find many other plants. Gorse and even harebells are common, but other **lime-loving species** are more unusual – frog and bee orchids grow here, as does the rarer musk.

Nutterswood, and the track becomes grassy as it goes beneath rock faces on the left, topped by another Iron Age fort.

Both upper and lower tracks lead up to the same point on Huddlestone's

A frosty morning on Cleeve Hill

Table, a level, grassy area which is a great viewpoint as well as being a good picnicking place.

At the top the path divides **C**. Fork left away from the wall. After about 300 yds (274m) a path crosses, coming from a gate to the right. Turn left and then keep ahead over another grassy path to come to yet another one coming from radio masts.

Turn left here to make for a lone tree protected by a paling **D**. From here the way lies across the golf course, the objective being the summit of Cleeve Hill, topped by a triangulation pillar and a view-indicator.

From the summit follow the sign-post on a level footpath heading north-east to pass a seat. From here the clubhouse can be clearly seen. The path passes a former quarry by tee 18, which has an information board explaining the geology of the strata exposed in the rock face. A few more minutes of easy walking takes you back to the clubhouse and car park. ●

The Iron Age earthworks scattered around Cleeve Common are easily explained today, as are the deep troughs lower down, caused by the spring line. However, our ancestors believed that both features were caused by sea erosion at the time when **Noah's Ark** was adrift in the Flood.

7 *Leckhampton Hill*

START Leckhampton Hill car park
DISTANCE 3½ miles (5.6km)
TIME 2 hours
PARKING At start
ROUTE FEATURES The gradients are not severe but there is a rocky staircase that may be slippery

Leckhampton is a suburb on the south side of Cheltenham and its hill is where much of the limestone used in building the elegant houses of its squares and terraces came from. In 1929 the town council bought the 400-acre (162 ha) hilltop to forestall further quarrying and since then it has become a favourite venue for locals and visitors alike. Certainly there is no finer viewpoint for the spa and many miles of surrounding countryside.

Leave the car park and turn right at the lane. When the lane begins to descend steeply leave it to the right on to a footpath with the Cotswold Way sign **A**.

A quarry, used as a car park, lies below the path which climbs gently with a wonderful view before you. The Devil's Chimney is best seen before you reach the top, lower paths giving excellent views of it.

Beyond the Chimney the topmost path rises to the summit, where there are sparse remains of an Iron Age fort. Keep to the top path which passes a view-indicator and then a triangulation pillar sited on the ramparts of the fort. A maze of paths covers this part of the hill.

Follow the path just to the left of

Can you guess how many people once huddled on the summit of the Devil's Chimney?

PUBLIC TRANSPORT None
REFRESHMENTS None on route
PUBLIC TOILETS None
ORDNANCE SURVEY MAPS Explorer 179 (Gloucester, Cheltenham & Stroud), Landranger 163 (Cheltenham & Cirencester)

the triangulation pillar, which goes through a spinney of pine trees to reach a surfaced drive **B**. Take the rough path to the left of this to follow a fence and continue to do this after a footpath junction by a group of ailing fir trees (the Cotswold Way follows the bridleway at this point, which is an equally attractive

Palaeontologists have been hammering fossils out of the exposed layers of **oolitic limestone** here for many years to the point where considerable damage has been caused. The top layer of limestone is known as ragstone and was used for walls, cottages and farm buildings. The best quality of material, freestone, is of finer grain and lies below the ragstone.

route). Either way, the views are compelling and the choice of paths is irrelevant as long as you stay near the top of the escarpment with pine trees in sight to the right.

After a stretch through dense undergrowth the pine trees end to the right and a footpath leaves up steps to Hartley Farm. Just after this

The Devil's Chimney

there is another junction **C** where a bridleway forks to the left. Take the footpath to the right (Cotswold Way) which begins a steady descent down a spur towards the main road, twisting through gorse.

There is a rocky staircase and a cycle barrier before the path reaches open land. Bear right along the

hedgerow and at the end turn left to a T-junction **D**

Turn right following the Cotswold Way sign and then right again at the road **E**. The mile (1.6km) of road-walking is easy and pleasant after the short initial climb. The quiet lane passes Hartley Farm and then soon reaches the Leckhampton Hill car park. ●

> The **Devil's Chimney** is a stone pillar made by 19th-century quarrymen who hazardously separated it from the cliff edge. It soon became a place where daring young men could show off their agility. Tradition used to be that a coin had to be left on the top to appease the devil. Climbing the chimney is forbidden today – not only because of the danger but also because of the damage that would be caused to the rock itself, already suffering from erosion.

Sezincote from Bourton-on-the-Hill

8

START Bourton-on-the-Hill
DISTANCE 3½ miles (5.6km)
TIME 2 hours
PARKING On-road parking on byway to south of A44
ROUTE FEATURES Grassy walking without severe gradients; some mud in wet weather

Bourton-on-the-Hill is a picture-book village when viewed from this walk, though it suffers from being bisected by a major road. The walk follows rights-of-way through meadows and parkland and passes Sezincote, a unique mansion with famous gardens in an idyllic setting.

From the telephone-box at the corner of Bourton-on-the-Hill's back street, walk a few steps westwards and then take the footpath on the left by Smithy Cottage – Bourton's blacksmith must have been prosperous to have such a house! Pass through a gate and descend by a wall to another one **A**.

Go left after this to follow the hedgerow and a small stream through three meadows before turning right at a line of oak trees on to an enclosed footpath **B**

which will be muddy after wet weather.

Turn left to walk by the side of a newly planted spinney to a stile that takes the path across a drive and to a footbridge into a small copse. After this the path continues to follow a stream towards a wood. Turn left to cross a footbridge **C** and then walk away from the

? *Can you spot something fearsome observing you on this pleasant walk?*

PUBLIC TRANSPORT Buses from Cirencester, Bourton-on-the-Water, Stow-on-the-Wold, Cheltenham, Chipping Campden and Moreton-in-Marsh. Tel. 01452 425543
REFRESHMENTS Pub in Bourton-on-the-Hill
PUBLIC TOILETS None
ORDNANCE SURVEY MAPS Outdoor Leisure 45 (The Cotswolds)

The dome of **Sezincote** and its orange-coloured stonework show that its builder had Indian connections. Sir Charles Cockerell made his fortune with the East India Company and began the house in 1805. The dome is said to have given the Prince Regent the idea for the Brighton Pavilion. Although the exterior is flamboyant, the interior is restrained and classical. However, the gardens are as spectacular as the outside of the house, and overall it makes Sezincote one of England's most appealing country-houses.

wood, keeping a hedge and ditch to the right.

Turn right at the end of the meadow on to a surfaced track and come to Upper Rye Farm. Pass to the left of the farm and turn right after a corrugated hay barn to reach the surfaced track coming away from the farm. This is easy walking through splendid country-side. Note the magnificent oak trees.

A short, steady climb takes the route up to the Keepers' Cottages.

Turn right 100 yds (91m) after these **D** before the cattle-grid on to a path by the side of a wood. Bear right away from the wood as the lake comes into view on the right. The right-of-way drops down to the meadow between the lake and the house.

After two gates close together the path turns right to follow a wooden fence. Keep ahead when this ends **E** to follow frequent waymarks through the beautiful park to a pair of wooden kissing-gates. Note the ridge-and-furrow patterns which at one point lie at right angles to one another.

St Laurence's Church has Norman piers even though it looks Perpendicular from the outside. **Bourton-on-the-Hill** has several houses that could almost claim to be mansions, most notably the early 18th-century Bourton House at the bottom end of the village and Manor Farmhouse (of the same period) at the top.

The path is obvious once Bourton-on-the-Hill comes into view, heading directly towards the church. There are grand houses on each flank of the village. The outward route is rejoined at the end of a wall and soon takes you back to the village. ●

Sezincote House

9 *Chastleton from Adlestrop*

This route is a delightful way of savouring the best Cotswold scenery without taxing gradients. It also allows you to see a splendid historic house and adjacent church. Keep a look out for foxes and deer.

START Adlestrop village hall at centre of village nearly opposite the shelter featuring the old station nameboard

DISTANCE 3½ miles (5.6km)

TIME 2 hours

PARKING At village hall (contribute to honesty box)

ROUTE FEATURES No taxing gradients. Because some of the tracks are used by horses, parts will be muddy after wet weather

This field was cultivated in strips in medieval times which has left characteristic **ridges and furrows**. Note how the moles prefer the ridges, probably because of the abundance of worms that are still enjoying the richness in the soil after centuries of organic farming.

Turn left out of the car park and then immediately left again on to a broad track that leads past a riding-school and then follows the edge of a field. After a gate bear left to cross a meadow diagonally.

Cross a stile in the bottom corner of the field by a stream, follow a fence for 50 yds (46m) and then climb the stile on the left by an oak tree. Follow the waymark and keep ahead at the footpath junction at a gateway **A**. The sadly derelict Hill Barn is to the left as the path climbs through a large meadow to a gateway. Pause to enjoy the view from here – Stow can be seen beyond the ruined barn.

? *What made the old railway station sign in Adlestrop so well known?*

Follow the Macmillan Way logo ('Across Country for Cancer Care') and cross a field to the corner of

PUBLIC TRANSPORT Tel. 01452 425543

REFRESHMENTS None

PUBLIC TOILETS None

ORDNANCE SURVEY MAPS Outdoor Leisure 45 (The Cotswolds)

Peasewell Wood **B**.
Here a gate opens on
to a track through an
oak avenue leading to
Chastleton House.
Note the pretty dove-
cote on the right.

Turn right to pass the
house and the church.
Follow the lane that
climbs and then
turns right
before a
cattle-grid.
At the
next

The dovecote at Chastleton

bend, where the road turns sharply left, keep ahead to climb a stile and join a path **C** between fields along the flank of Adlestrop Hill. There are superb views over the outward part of the route to Stow and beyond. Note that there is no sign of a bridleway as marked on the map, everyone follows the track.

Keep ahead along the edge of a wood – you may well see a fox or deer here. Turn right before a gate going into the wood **D**. Follow the edge of the wood and then a hedge to reach a stile and gate near

Chastleton House was built between 1607 and 1612 by Walter Jones, a wealthy lawyer. Chastleton is unique mainly because the Jones family were never affluent and seldom improved the house or its furnishings. The National Trust sought to preserve its unique atmosphere, even keeping forty-year-old jars of preserved fruit. The beautiful garden preserves Jacobean features. Note that at peak periods booking is necessary (tel. 01608 674355).

the corner of the field.

Go through the gate to a path through newly planted woodland (Long Drive). This soon gives way to a belt of more established trees. The path then drops down and may be muddy before it reaches a road.

Turn right along the road and, where it bends left and begins to descend steeply, keep ahead **E** on the drive to Fern Farm. When the drive bends left at a 'Keep to public footpath' sign **F**, turn left on to a grass track running between fields.

Turn left at the bottom of the field to reach the road. Turn right to pass the bus shelter and its well-known sign to return to the village hall, or spend a little time exploring the beautiful Cotswold village. ●

Adlestrop countryside

Haresfield Beacon

10

START Shortwood car park, on minor road between Painswick and Haresfield

DISTANCE 3½ miles (5.6km)

TIME 2½ hours

PARKING At start

ROUTE FEATURES Some climbing to viewpoints, ridge walk, steep descent

Many people park their cars and walk ¼ mile (400m) across springy turf to the view-indicator, admire the view and return to the car park, congratulating themselves on the exercise. This route demands more effort, taking you through woodland before climbing to Haresfield Beacon. Then there is a ridge walk and another short climb to get to the view-indicator where you can feel pity for the ordinary mortals who have come here the conventional way.

From the car park turn right to follow the path to the left of the wall that is the boundary of National Trust land. Keep the wall to the right as the path follows the edge of a field and reaches a road. Climb a stile and turn left, bearing left at a road junction at Bird in Hand and passing Stoneridge Farm before taking the footpath on the right that begins by the bus-stop **A**.

Walk across the large field, heading for a white post to the right of the radio masts. Cross the road into woodland and keep ahead to descend steeply – the writer found a stick helpful in managing this safely – following yellow arrows stencilled on tree trunks. Towards the bottom the gradient eases. Turn left **B** on to the track that is part of the Cotswold Way.

? *Can you find the old inscription and what it tells you to seek after your bucketful?*

PUBLIC TRANSPORT Tel. 01452 425543

REFRESHMENTS None on route

PUBLIC TOILETS None

ORDNANCE SURVEY MAPS Explorer 179 (Gloucester, Cheltenham & Stroud), Landranger 163 (Cheltenham & Cirencester)

The going now becomes easy on a pleasant bridleway on the edge of Stockend Wood. When it joins a lane, keep ahead on it as it descends for almost ¼ mile (400m) before turning left **C** on to a bridleway signposted to Haresfield Beacon, where it levels. Note Cliff Well, on the left, with a curiously bent cross on top of the well-house.

A steady climb follows. Where the track bends left there is a granite memorial stone that

commemorates the raising of the Siege of Gloucester by Royalists in 1643 that also testifies to the ancient importance of the track.

After this the walking is easier and the track soon reaches a lane at Ringhill Farm. Turn left and, after 50 yds (46m), right **D** on to a footpath following the Cotswold Way logo past two gates and on to a track climbing up the flank of Ring Hill. Just before the top a stile takes the path on to the

Memorial stone near Cliff Well

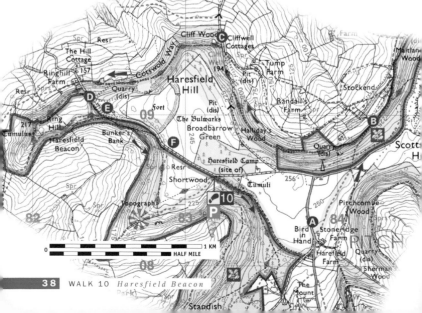

triangulation pillar that gives a wonderful view across the Vale of Gloucester and the Forest of Dean to the Brecon Beacons.

Turn sharp left from the pillar to negotiate the ramparts of the Iron Age fort and follow the ridge eastwards to a stile. A hoard of 3,000 Roman coins was once discovered near the remains of the fort. The path is very well trodden and soon reaches the road **E**.

Haresfield Beacon

However, turn right a few steps before reaching a National Trust moneybox to descend steps and reach a path that follows a wall. There are fine views to the right and then a steady climb to a footpath junction **F**. Bear right across the grass to head for the view-indicator, which from the distance looks like an upturned drum.

The topograph turns out to be a remarkable work in bronze that shows the rivers and hills of the surrounding area. On a good day you can see the Sugar Loaf Mountain near Abergavenny from here, more than 30 miles (48km) distant. Turn left away from the topograph on the most obvious path to return to the Shortwood car park. ●

Haresfield village is most famous for having once been the home of John Prichard, whose story inspired **Beatrix Potter** with the story of the Tailor of Gloucester. Mr Prichard was commissioned to make the Lord Mayor of Gloucester a new waistcoat. He cut out the material and left it on his workbench overnight. The next morning he found the garment had been completed and attributed this to the work of fairies. Beatrix Potter used to stay at neighbouring Harescombe, heard the story and modelled her drawing of the tailor on the son of the coachman there.

11 *Minchinhampton Common*

START Market House, Minchinhampton
DISTANCE 4 miles (6.4km)
TIME 2½ hours
PARKING Minchinhampton
ROUTE FEATURES Good going on footpaths, quiet lanes and grass

Minchinhampton is a large village on the south-west edge of the Cotswolds where lovely old houses huddle around a picturesque Market House and beautiful church. It occupies level ground between two valleys important for their woollen mills, a trade carried on here from the 17th to late 19th century. The village common is the largest one surviving in the area, a plateau giving good grassy walking and stunning views to north and west.

From the Market House (1698) walk up Bell Lane past Holy Trinity Church. Turn right to pass the east end of the church and follow the churchyard wall along the eastern side of the common. Bear right to the corner of the common at the end of Butt Street.

Cross over the main road into The Knapp and after 100 yds (91m) take the footpath on the left **A** that passes the site of a radio mast (soon to be erected). A stone stile takes the path across a driveway to an enclosed path with paddocks on each side.

Turn left when you come to the edge of the escarpment over-looking Besbury Common and enjoy the wonderful views north-wards of winding, wooded valleys and rolling hills from strategically placed seats. Like Minchin-hampton Common, this part of Besbury Common is in the care of the National Trust.

PUBLIC TRANSPORT Tel. 01452 425543
REFRESHMENTS Pubs in Minchinhampton
PUBLIC TOILETS Opposite Minchinhampton church in Bell Lane
ORDNANCE SURVEY MAPS Explorer 168 (Stroud, Tetbury & Malmsbury), Landranger 163 (Cheltenham & Cirencester)

The path joins a quiet lane. Go right at a T-junction **B** down a hill to pass the Old Weaver's House. The lane ends at a main road by the gates on to Minchinhampton Common. Keep ahead for 100 yds (91m) and pass Burleigh House before bearing right down Burleigh Lane. There are more fine views from this road, also usually free of traffic.

Minchinhampton

Keep ahead at the main road and climb to the common. By the Burleigh village sign **C** bear right across the open common, initially heading for a black-and-white post on top of a prominent mound on the skyline. From here cross a short stretch of uneven ground to reach the road with a large pit close to the right.

> **?** *To what local trade does Holy Trinity Church owe its size?*

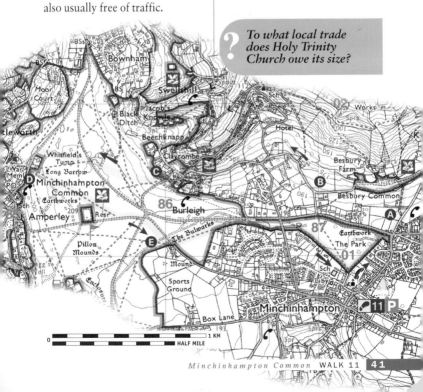

View from Besbury Common

Cross the next part of the common heading westwards towards a large building half hidden by trees. Pass to the right of the building (a tall semi-detached house) and cross the road for a view of Nailsworth valley.

Turn back to the road and walk past the war memorial and cross to the bus shelter that has a weather vane on its roof **D**. From here go across the common to follow a line of earthworks (part of the extensive Amberley Camp, an Iron Age hillfort) towards a reservoir –

Holy Trinity Church was a Norman church enlarged in the 12th century, but its most glorious feature – the south transept with its enormous window – dates from early in the 14th century. The tower owes its appearance to an unsafe spire that was abbreviated in 1563 when the delightful coronet was added to compensate.

distinctive with a stone wall topped by grey railings. Pass to the left of it to come to the middle one of three signposts standing by a point where six roads meet.

Walk by the side of the road signposted to Minchinhampton town centre and, where The Bulwarks cross it **E**, turn left to follow the ramparts and deep ditch towards another road, making for a large house with a flagpole (Seymour House, a copy of a colonial house in India built in 1890).

Minchinhampton Common covers 580 acres (235 ha) and belongs to the National Trust. Although rights of way are shown on the map, the paths are mainly indistinct on the ground. This does not matter much since walkers have completely free access and in good conditions there are plenty of landmarks to assist navigation.

Follow the wall with the Bulwarks – an enclosed area of 600 acres (243 ha) of defence works dug in the Iron Age against the Romans' advance – and the road to the left. Cross a road and continue to follow the wall on the perimeter of the common. Holy Trinity Church, with its unique coronet, is soon to be seen ahead and the way back to the village centre is clear. ●

Snowshill

START Snowshill
DISTANCE 4 miles (6.4km)
TIME 2½ hours
PARKING Village car park on road to Broadway
ROUTE FEATURES Paths may be muddy after wet weather or if they have been overused by riders. Although there are short sections uphill, none of the gradients is unduly taxing

12

Snowshill is famous for its manor, once the home of the eccentric Charles Wade, and as a beauty spot, perched halfway up a hill on the northern edge of the Cotswolds. The delightfully varied route uses footpaths, bridleways and lanes, all of which give splendid views of the village and surrounding countryside.

Cottages in Snowshill

🖉 Turn right out of the car park and fork right to descend to the village, passing the back of Snowshill Manor, then the pub and the church. Bear right, noting the

wall on the right embellished with built-in stone balls and triangles.

A footpath leaves to the right but continue climbing the lane, turning right at the junction near the top. There is a fine view to the right as you pass Sheepscombe Farm. Turn right after this, and after 150 yds (46m) go left through **Ⓐ** an iron gate and climb through the meadow towards the upper part of Littleworth Wood. A stile, hidden

? *Why would witches have approved of Littleworth Wood?*

PUBLIC TRANSPORT None
REFRESHMENTS Pub in Snowshill
PUBLIC TOILETS None
ORDNANCE SURVEY MAPS Outdoor Leisure 45 (The Cotswolds)

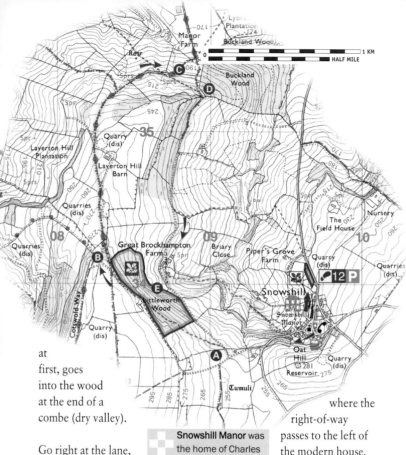

at
first, goes
into the wood
at the end of a
combe (dry valley).

Go right at the lane, which follows the top of the wood. Bear right at the end of the wood to follow the Cotswold Way waymarks **B**.

There is an incomparable 180° view as you approach Laverton Hill Barn,

Snowshill Manor was the home of Charles Wade, a human magpie, who collected curious objects from all over the world. Many of them remain in the beautiful house, which Wade presented to the National Trust in 1951. The manor dates from the early 16th century (with later additions and alterations) while the wonderful terraced garden was laid out in 1919.

where the right-of-way passes to the left of the modern house.

Broadway is well seen ahead as the track swings right and begins to descend. Remain on the Cotswold Way when a bridleway leaves to the left. Broadway Tower can be seen ahead.

Go through a metal gate and follow a fence – Buckland church is seen to the left. Just before a distinctive stone gate-post there is a stile to the left, and a footpath leaves at the gatepost **C** to climb past a waymark post towards the lower edge of Buckland Wood.

Cross a stile at the corner of the wood and turn right on to a bridle-way **D**. There is an isolated cottage to the left with Snowshill ahead in its picturesque setting. The track is surfaced after the driveway leading to the cottage.

Locals pronounce Snowshill's name as **'Snozzle'**. St Barnabas' Church was completely rebuilt in 1864, only the font surviving from the medieval building.

Keep on the lane at Great Brockhampton Farm, but turn sharp left on to the drive coming from it and cross the stile into the paddock on the right **E**. Follow the paddock fence to join a well-trodden path that climbs to a stile giving on to an enclosed path.

A stile leads to a pleasant stretch of grassy walking to pass a pond to the left. The path joins a driveway climbing back to Snowshill. Retrace your steps to the car park. ●

Snowshill from the south

13 *Batsford from Blockley*

START Blockley post office at centre of village
DISTANCE 4½ miles (7.2km)
TIME 2½ hours
PARKING On road parking by green at village centre
ROUTE FEATURES Short, steep sections; going may be muddy in places

Trees must be the theme of this route which takes the walker around the perimeter of one of Britain's most notable arboretums. Batsford's trees have to be admired from afar unless you pay for entry, but footpaths pass by many native trees that have astonishing girth and height. The strenuous sections of the route are separated by sections on a plateau giving outstanding views in all directions.

From the post office go into the churchyard and walk past the east end of the church, bearing right and passing the Manor House before reaching the road at the bottom. Turn right and after Lower Brook House turn left **A** on to a bridleway signposted to Pasture Farm.

? *Blockley once had six mills. What cloth were they supplying (it was not wool)?*

After almost ½ mile (800m) fork right off the track **B** to go behind a large farm shed and continue climbing the edge of the field with the hedge to the right. This is waymarked as part of the Donnington Way, a footpath sponsored by the famous village brewery.

PUBLIC TRANSPORT Buses from Chipping Campden and Moreton-in-Marsh. Tel. 01452 425543
REFRESHMENTS Tearoom and pub at Blockley, tearoom at Batsford Arboretum in season
PUBLIC TOILETS At start
ORDNANCE SURVEY MAPS Outdoor Leisure 45 (The Cotswolds)

The waymarks are black spots in white circles. It is worth pausing on the lengthy ascent to take in views of the village and countryside.

A glance at the map shows the abundance of ancient earthworks in the vicinity, and the rough ground here, where the path follows electric lines to a gate at the top corner of the meadow, may be man-made.

The path follows a row of grand trees at the top. Keep ahead after a footpath crosses the bridleway with a wall and hedge to the left. It reaches a lane after crossing a field.

The lane descends steadily and passes Batsford estate offices and the former school. Keep ahead over two crossroads (both roads to the right end at Batsford

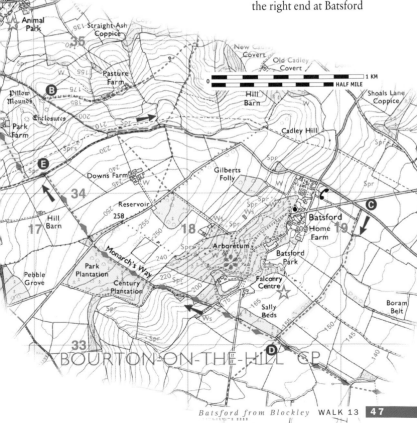

The centre of Blockley village

church). About 100 yds (91m) past the second crossroads, turn right **C** on to a path enclosed by young oak trees.

Batsford Park is to the right, and walkers may see red deer and the smaller muntjacs as well as birds of prey, whose flying skills are often demonstrated in the park. Turn right at a footpath junction **D** to join the Monarch's Way.

The path follows the edge of pastures corrugated by medieval ridge and furrow agriculture. Some of the furrows will be wet after rainfall. Cross the drive into the arboretum by a cottage and climb to a stile. Turn left on to the drive on the other side to follow the perimeter wall and enjoy views towards Bourton-on-the-Hill.

Batsford Arboretum was created by Lord Redesdale who came to the estate in 1886 having served as a diplomat in Tokyo and China. There are now more than a thousand varieties of trees on display, the colours being particularly spectacular in spring (azaleas, cherries and rhododendron) and autumn. For opening times tel. 01608 650722 or 01386 700409 (weekends).

Turn right at a 'Private' sign and climb to the wall where a muddy footpath climbs steeply through Century Plantation, with the wall close to the right. There is a good view back from near the top, and you go past a curious stage-like structure before reaching a road.

Blockley is a delightfully haphazard village with picturesque cottages of all ages spread about the church and neighbouring green.

Cross the road to a well-used footpath that soon begins to descend towards Blockley. A T-junction **E** provides a superb viewpoint for the village and its countryside. Turn left here and after 100 yds (91m) climb a stile on the right to head down over grazing land in the direction of Blockley church.

Pass to the left of Park Farm and climb a stile before crossing a drive and passing a pond to drop down to a gate in the right-hand corner of the field. A short length of track takes the path to a road. Turn right to retrace your steps back to the starting point.

The view of Blockley from point E

14 *Lost village of Widford from Burford*

START Burford car park
DISTANCE 4½ miles (7.2km)
TIME 2 hours
PARKING At start
ROUTE FEATURES Riverside walking with a few gradients and a succession of stiles; riverside may be wet

Burford is one of the most interesting, historic and beautiful of Cotswold towns and any new visitor is recommended to explore it thoroughly. The route begins by following the River Windrush to Widford, where there was a sizeable village until the Black Death. Today there are two farms, a cottage, mill and tiny medieval chapel. After a lovely climb up a hidden valley the walk takes you back via Fulbrook (where it detours to pass the manor house at Westhall Hill).

From the car park cross the bridge and turn left at the main road. Go left again opposite the magnificent Great House – like many Burford houses, its classical façade is misleading and screens a house of an earlier time.

Leave the town by a pleasant road lined with picturesque cottages. Soon the houses end and you can look left to where a loop of the River Windrush rejoins the main river.

There are about 200 yds (183m) of road walking without a footway before you turn left **A** over a stile to join a footpath through

> **?** What connects Red Indians with Henry VIII's barber?

PUBLIC TRANSPORT Tel. 01452 425543
REFRESHMENTS Pubs and cafés at Burford, pubs at Fulbrook
PUBLIC TOILETS Burford
ORDNANCE SURVEY MAPS Outdoor Leisure 45 (The Cotswolds)

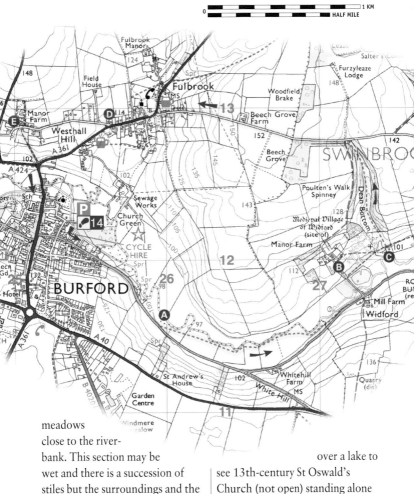

meadows
close to the river-
bank. This section may be
wet and there is a succession of
stiles but the surroundings and the
wildlife provides constant interest.
Too soon the path climbs to a road.

Join the road for a short way and
then turn left to cross the river at
Widford Mill. Look to the right

over a lake to
see 13th-century St Oswald's
Church (not open) standing alone
by the river, the only building of
the medieval village to survive.
Widford occupied the site of a
Roman villa (a fragment of
mosaic survives in the chancel of
St Oswald's) and was probably

abandoned at the time of the Black Death.

Turn right after the lake on to a footpath signposted to Swinbrook **B**, crossing a cattle-grid. The track passes the church and goes over another cattle-grid. Turn left **C** before the isolated Shepherd's Cottage to walk up Dean Bottom, a lovely dry valley (though it may hardly merit this description at first) with woods on both sides above the rich grass.

Burford was established as a wool town in 1088 when the first of its guilds was formed to protect the trade. It continued to grow until the 17th century when Sir Lawrence Tanfield bought the lordship of the manor and successfully challenged the power in the independent hands of the aldermen and the guilds. Even so Burford continued to be a busy place until the main road was diverted in 1812 so that coaching traffic could avoid its steep hills.

This part of the walk seems too short before the stile at the top is reached. Turn left on to Blacksmith's Lane – there are good views after Beech Grove Farm, where the descent into Fulbrook begins.

The Mason's Arms is just to the right when you come to the main road. Turn left to pass the church

Burford in spring

Westhall – the manor-house

and then fork right **D** into a cul-de-sac about 200 yds (183m) before Fulbrook's other pub, the Carpenters' Arms. The road climbs Westhall Hill giving excellent views of Burford. To the right there is a remarkable cluster of beautiful old buildings surrounding the 16th-century manor-house (not open to the public) with its distinctive archway. The duckpond completes a perfect scene.

You will have to walk back for a few yards after this to find a footpath on the right **E** that begins by a garage with green doors. The way leads down, steeply at the finish, to reach the main road at the roundabout by Burford bridge – note the wartime pillbox at the bottom.

Only lower parts of the tower and west end survive of the church that served Burford in Norman times. After this, bits were added at various levels and in a variety of styles. Nevertheless, **St John the Baptist's Church** is a treasure-house to students of church architecture who love the problems it presents. There is a splendid south porch and a wonderful display of monuments. Look for graffiti on the font scratched by a Roundhead kept prisoner in 1649.

Cross the bridge and then turn left up Lawrence Lane to the church. Follow the footpath round the churchyard to a lane and pass almshouses founded in 1457 to return to the car park. ●

15 *Farmington from Northleach*

Northleach was one of the Cotswold's wealthiest towns in the 15th century, and the magnificent church is the testament to this prosperity. The walk takes in the attractive countryside to the east of the town where rolling fields and lush streamside pastures surround the tiny village of Farmington.

START Northleach market square
DISTANCE 5 miles (8km). Shorter version 4 miles (7.2km)
TIME 3 hours (2 hours for shorter route)
PARKING At start
ROUTE FEATURES May be short sections across cultivated land; lack of waymarks

From the market square, walk through the churchyard and turn left almost opposite the porch. Once outside the churchyard turn left and then go right into Mill View. Turn left before the school **A** on to a footpath that crosses a playing-field making for the children's playground.

Go through the kissing-gate at the end of the tennis-courts to walk through meadows to a lane, reached from the top corner of the last meadow. Turn right and climb uphill.

Just after reaching the crest, turn left into a cul-de-sac. Keep ahead through the gate at the postbox when the lane bends right at Upper End **B**. Bear right to go down to the

PUBLIC TRANSPORT Buses from Cheltenham, Cirencester, Moreton-in-Marsh, Oxford and Stow-on-the-Wold. Tel. 01452 425543
REFRESHMENTS Pubs and tearoom in Northleach
PUBLIC TOILETS In the market square
ORDNANCE SURVEY MAPS Outdoor Leisure 45 (The Cotswolds)

? *What are the rats enjoying in the Saints' porch?*

bottom end of the lake and cross the bridge over the outfall stream.

Climb the steep track on the other side and go through the metal gate at the top to a farm track. When this goes to the right, walk ahead along a path along a field edge.

After a metal gate at the end of the field **C** turn left and cross land to a stile leading into a belt of conifers. Cross the main road and continue on another field-edge path that heads towards Farmington.

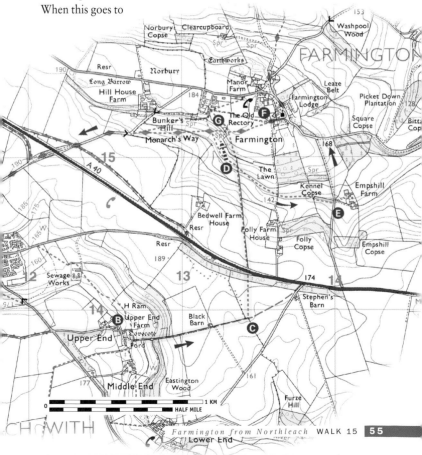

The path descends to cross a stream by an iron gate. A few steps further on there is a footpath junction **D**.

For the short route keep ahead alongside the fence and then by the edge of the field (there is a drop to the left) to a stile **G** *on the left bearing a Monarch's Way emblem.*

To continue on the main route, go through the gate on the right on to

Stone from the quarries at **Farmington** was sent to London by road and river to rebuild the city after the Great Fire of 1666. The parish was one of the first in Gloucestershire to be enclosed (in 1713) and the walls put up at this time with stone from the same quarries remain in place today.

The Lawn, a beautiful expanse of pasture descending to a brook. The right-of-way follows the left bank of the stream until the final field, where it crosses the stream and then reaches a wooden gate giving on to a lane.

Turn left **E** and then, after ½ mile (800m) of easy climbing, left again to Farmington's unpretentious little church. Take the track along

Northleach

St Peter's Church, Farmington

the south side of the churchyard following the Monarch's Way. Keep ahead when the track divides. The footpath also divides here **F**.

Fork left and head across the large field, keeping to the left of the electric lines. By the time you reach the far side you should be about 100 yds (91m) distant from them and will see a shed ahead. Cross the stile here **G**, descend to the bottom of the valley and cross the stream by a footbridge (there is another crossing-point further up-stream). From the second bridge climb up

the field to its top edge, following the power lines again. Here there is a track that reaches the road by a group of young conifers.

The quiet lane passes beneath the A40. Leave it to the right on to a footpath close to a 7.5-tonne restriction sign **H**.

The path descends through trees and then is enclosed through housing. Keep ahead down MacArthur Road, turning left at the bottom into Doctor's Lane, a broad alleyway that leads to Northleach market-place. ●

> **Northleach** had a brief period of prosperity in the 15th and 16th centuries, when its Church of Saints Peter and Paul was enlarged and beautified, the only hints of the earlier Norman building being the ridge-line of a previous roof on the east side of the tower. The brasses to the memory of Northleach's medieval merchants are outstanding.

16 *Woodchester Park*

START National Trust car park off Nympsfield – Stroud road

DISTANCE 5 miles (8km)

TIME 3 hours

PARKING At start

ROUTE FEATURES Paths through the National Trust estate are well maintained, a few gradients may be taxing; picnic tables

Situated barely 3 miles (4.8km) to the south of Stroud, Woodchester Park is one of the Cotswolds' secret places. The amazing mansion, in High Gothic style where everything is made of stone, has never been lived in yet stands more or less intact after more than 130 years. The surrounding park has five lakes – modestly called ponds – that often have the appearance of Scottish lochs, the steep sides of their valley clothed with pine trees.

The steps that descend from the car park take you to a woodland track that steadily drops down to a delightful pastoral valley. Follow orange waymarks and fork left when the track divides at the bottom **A**.

The track goes behind the Mansion, passing remains of outbuildings on the left and the remains of the former terraced gardens to the right. The climb continues through woodland and at last there is a glimpse of a narrow lake to the right – this is Brick Kiln Pond, first in the series of five. Originally all the ponds were set amidst

PUBLIC TRANSPORT None

REFRESHMENTS Pub in Bourton-on-the-Hill

PUBLIC TOILETS At Mansion when open to public

ORDNANCE SURVEY MAPS Explorer 168 (Stroud, Tetbury & Malmsbury), Landranger 163 (Cheltenham & Cirencester)

? *What will you not find at Woodchester Mansion because Viollet-le-Duc deplored it?*

parkland and pasture. In time the National Trust hope to open up these landscapes again.

Woodchester Mansion is a romantic building. In 1845 William Leigh bought the estate (embracing five parishes) for £100,000. He had recently become a Roman Catholic and commissioned designs for two projects – a country-house for himself and a church and monastery on a different site.

Pugin and Charles Francis Hansom produced drawings for **Woodchester Mansion** but their work was rejected in favour of a 21-year-old local architect, Benjamin Bucknall. He was a disciple of Viollet-le-Duc, an expert on Gothic architecture. On Leigh's death in 1873, after sixteen years' work, the project was abandoned overnight, leaving scaffolding erected and tools where they lay. Fortunately, the roof had been completed. Visitors may tour the house at weekends in summer. For opening times tel. 01453 750455.

Keep following orange waymarks as the track descends and continue to follow them on the main track when the red route leaves to the left, above Honeywell Pond. After 200 yds (183m) bear right as the track descends, steeply at first and then more gently. At the end of Middle Pond, the Old Kennels can be

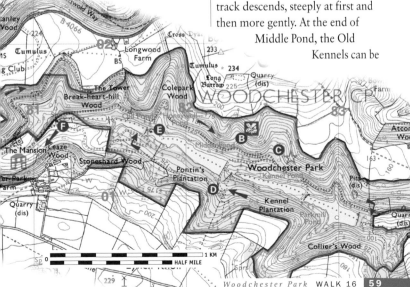

seen to the right on the far side of a broad causeway. Keep ahead **B**, now following the red waymark.

The red route goes to the left **C** at a T-junction. Leave it by turning right on a track that soon gives views of Kennel Pond, separated from Parkmill Pond by a narrow causeway.

The Boathouse

Turn right to cross the end of Parkmill Pond to follow red waymarks again. A waterfall can be seen some distance up the lake from the dam. Turn right again to walk up the track on the south side of Parkmill Pond. This side of the lake is much more enclosed by trees.

On the far side of this a kissing-gate opens on to a more narrow path with wooden steps and plank-walks over difficult ground.

The picturesque Boathouse stands by the causeway separating Old Pond from Middle Pond **E**. Cross the causeway and turn left along a shoreline path that leads up to a driveway used earlier. After about 300 yds (274m) keep ahead to follow orange/red waymarks to go through a gate **F** on to a track that will take you past the Mansion and on to the main track that climbs steadily to the car park. ●

Bear right to pass The Old Kennels, an open shed with picnic tables, but do not cross the causeway. Turn left **D** to continue along the south side of Middle Pond, joining a good path crossing an open grassy area, a former poplar plantation.

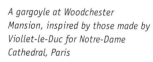

A gargoyle at Woodchester Mansion, inspired by those made by Viollet-le-Duc for Notre-Dame Cathedral, Paris

The Slaughters from Bourton-on-the-Water

START Bourton-on-the-Water church

DISTANCE 5 miles (8km). Shorter version 4 miles (6.4km)

TIME 2½ hours (2 hours for shorter route)

PARKING Public car parks in Bourton

ROUTE FEATURES Stretches may be muddy; steady climb out of valley

17

Upper and Lower Slaughter have featured on countless calendars through the years, the pictures usually showing honey-coloured cottages and the quaint foot-bridges that span the tiny River Eye. The walk offers many different vistas of the villages, while Bourton-on-the-Water, hardly less famous, also reveals an unexpected beauty spot.

 From the church turn left along Bourton's main street and then cross the River Windrush by the bridge opposite the Old Manse Hotel. Pass the Old Bakery and turn right on to a narrow footpath **A** (the start of the Windrush Way) where the road divides at The Warren Restaurant. The twisting path suddenly emerges into a lovely riverside meadow – a delightful surprise that must be Bourton's best-kept secret. All too soon the path by the river reaches the road. Turn left to come to the A429 (Fosse Way).

> **?** *What group of people built the Fosse Way?*

Cross the main road by the bridge that bears a plaque showing the badge of the Second Legion, who were responsible for building the

---

PUBLIC TRANSPORT Buses from Cirencester, Moreton-in-Marsh, Stow-on-the-Wold, Cheltenham and Northleach. Stagecoach tel. 01242 522021, Pulhams buses tel. 01451 820369

REFRESHMENTS Teashop at The Mill, Lower Slaughter, in season; pubs and teashops in Bourton

PUBLIC TOILETS At village centre next to Edinburgh Woollen Mills shop

ORDNANCE SURVEY MAPS Outdoor Leisure 45 (The Cotswolds)

Fosse Way. Take the footpath on the east side of the Windrush, which at first follows it closely through a meadow. At the end of the meadow the path follows a field-edge track and rises to skirt a wood. If it has been wet and used by horses this short stretch of the route may be muddy. It is hard to see exactly where the path crossed the former Cheltenham to Chipping Norton railway line, but soon after this the path divides. Turn right on to the Gloucestershire Way **B**, turning your back to the River Windrush and beginning a climb the side of the valley.

After about ½ mile (800m) look for a metal gate on the right **C** that marks the start of another bridleway heading across a field (part of the Macmillan Way). Cross a road and continue on the bridleway, looking down to Bourton on the right and then to Lower Slaughter ahead. The bridleway comes to a crossways **D**.

The best way of seeing **Upper Slaughter** is on foot as car parking is practically non-existent. The footpaths on the return leg of the walk go through 'the slough' that gives the village its name, though the boggy area has been made into comparatively well-drained water meadows. The village is built around the site of a Norman castle, and the church dates from the same era, though this is disguised by 19th-century restoration.

Manor Hotel that dates from the 17th century and once served as the rectory. Pass the road to Guiting Power and turn right **E** into Upper Slaughter village, passing the church in a beautiful position set back from the cottages surrounding a small square. Bear left to pass the former village school where the famous view of the River Eye and the little bridges is revealed.

If you wish to take the shorter route, not visiting Upper Slaughter, keep ahead to the centre of Lower Slaughter. Turn right to follow the river and reach **G**.

To continue on the main route, turn left along the lane, admiring an ever-changing vista of Lower Slaughter, the church distinctive with the top of its spire dressed with new stone. Keep ahead when you reach a T-junction. Now you can see Upper Slaughter and the Lords of the

Cross the river: you may like to take the riverside footpath if dry conditions prevail (but avoid it if it is at all wet – the path is becoming eroded). Otherwise follow the road that runs parallel, turn left before the bridge and climb 100 yds (91m) up the road. Where it swings left, go through an iron gate **F** into a meadow and bear right to find another iron gate that takes the path on through a long meadow. There is a

Bourton-on-the-Water

fine view of the hotel across a pond.

A kissing-gate at the end of the meadow gives on to a riverside path leading into Lower Slaughter. Turn right at the road to reach the mill (that houses a museum) and then turn left to walk by the river through the village. Bear right almost opposite the church to continue on the left-hand bank of the river for about 100 yds (91m) by the road. Take the footpath on the right to leave the road and then keep ahead (now leaving the river) when a footpath goes off to the left.

Bourton-on-the-Water is famous for its series of bridges across the little River Windrush and the abundant blossom that turns the village green pink in spring. Visitors enjoy attractions such as the model village and Birdland.

After a metal gate **G**, bear left on the surfaced footpath that follows a hedge at first and then crosses a large field to reach the main road almost opposite the Coach and Horses. Turn right, and then, after 100 yds (91m), left into Bourton.

Pass Meadow Way on the left and, where the road bends right, take the footpath on the right **H** past a bungalow named Altamara. The footpath goes between a school and its playing-field and soon reaches the church. ●

Lower Slaughter

Winchcombe and Hailes Abbey

18

START Winchcombe – top of Castle Street

DISTANCE 5 miles (8km)

TIME 3 hours

PARKING On-street parking in Winchcombe or car park near Library

ROUTE FEATURES Comparatively easy going outward but the return is more demanding with steady climbs and muddy descents

This is a walk of several options, all of them attractive. The way to Hailes Abbey is along Puck Pit Lane (which proves to be as charming as its name suggests) and then by field paths. The leg up Salter's Lane and Fluke's Hill is more demanding with steady climbs and muddy descents. The beautiful pastures and woodland that the path goes through, together with far-reaching views, makes the effort worthwhile.

🖊 Turn down Castle Street by the White Hart and cross the concealed bridge that takes the road over the little River Isbourne. Turn left up an alleyway **Ⓐ**, following the Gloucestershire Way sign.

A kissing-gate takes the path into a riverside meadow with the medieval pattern of ridge-and-furrow cultivation clearly visible.

❓ Who was Puck?

Cross a footbridge and walk through two more meadows to a road. Bear right to follow the main road for 100 yds (91m) before turning right by the 30 mph sign into Puck Pit Lane **Ⓑ**.

This lovely byway is part of the Cotswold Way and gives views over fields and woodland. Once English main roads were like this! The lane ends at a pair of gates with stiles.

Cross a meadow heading to the left of a rusty-roofed cowshed and go

PUBLIC TRANSPORT Tel. 01452 425543

REFRESHMENTS Pubs and tearooms in Wincombe

PUBLIC TOILETS At Winchcombe and Hailes Abbey

ORDNANCE SURVEY MAPS Outdoor Leisure 45 (The Cotswolds)

Hailes Abbey (English Heritage, tel. 01242 602398) was founded in 1246 by Richard, Earl of Cornwall, as thanks after having been saved from shipwreck. Cistercian monks were brought from Beaulieu to run the abbey, which quickly became wealthy and powerful. This was helped by its famous relic, a phial of Holy Blood that attracted pilgrims from near and far. Chaucer's Pardoner mentions it in his Canterbury Tale. Only parts of the cloisters survive, though the other abbey buildings are marked on the ground, and there is a fascinating museum.

over a footbridge **C** into another meadow. There are views of lovely countryside to the left as you cross the next field to a kissing-gate near the lower corner, where the ground quickly becomes muddy after wet weather.

Walk through the long meadow – a footpath crosses from the left – to reach a gate at the far end. From here the right-of-way goes across a field to a field-edge track that leads to a wide farm track. Turn left on to this and turn right at the lane. After 150 yds (46m) the Cotswold Way leaves to the left **D** – follow it for ¼ mile (400m) to Hailes Abbey.

After your visit to the abbey, return to the lane and turn left (here named Salter's Lane; it is a continuation of the ancient Salt Way). The climb is easy at first but the way becomes steadily steeper as the lane passes Haile on the Hill and approaches woods. After about 20 minutes of

Puck Pit Lane

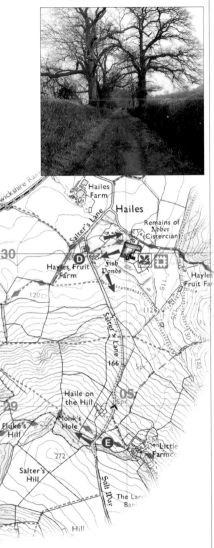

exertion, turn right through an iron gate near the top just before trees **E**.

The route again becomes part of the Gloucestershire Way – a lovely path along the flank of Fluke's Hill. Turn left when the path divides at a weighted gate and climb a steep slope to a stile into a wood. Steps lead down an equally steep bank. There follows a lovely section of grassy walking, descending gently and looking for a gate to the right before you reach the trees at the end of the long meadow.

From the gate the path descends another steep slope where there are flights of steps to help (but the going may still be slippery). Better

No stones are standing now of the great Benedictine **abbey** that dominated **Winchcombe**. It was founded by Kenulph, King of Mercia, in 811. After his son Kenelm was murdered by his wicked sister (who had her eyes torn out in an act of divine intervention) the abbey attracted crowds of pilgrims who believed that Kenelm's shrine had powerful holy properties. In 1539 the abbey was dissolved and the land and buildings given to the Seymours of Sudeley Castle. St Peter's Church was built about 1460 when the abbey was in its heyday. It has a fine tower, broad nave and beautiful organ case.

grassy walking follows with views of Winchcombe from near the first of a series of metal kissing-gates.

Cross a lane **F** and pass a huge oak tree in a pasture. The right-of-way (diverted to pass to the left of Stancombe Farm) is well marked by large plates of white plastic. When the diversion ends, head for Winchcombe across a large field.

Salt has been a vital commodity in England throughout history to preserve food through winter and spring. Most salt originated from Droitwich, and the Salt Way passed through the Cotswolds from Worcester to reach the Thames at Lechlade.

Turn left at a lane and after 50 yds (46m) go through a wooden gate on the right to cross the water meadow diagonally to the end of the alley-way used at the beginning of the route. At the road, turn right to return to the centre of the village of Winchcombe.

Cottages at Winchcombe

Guiting Wood

19

START Guiting Power
DISTANCE 6 miles (9.7km)
TIME 3½ hours
PARKING Village hall car park, Guiting Power (near church)
ROUTE FEATURES Some gradients and muddy ground through woodland

An advantage of this route is that you may like to undertake it in two parts – there is a small, isolated car park on the way just off Critchford Lane where you can leave the car close to the halfway point. The walk will be particularly rewarding in spring or autumn when foliage is at its most colourful. If you have to ask for directions note that Guiting is pronounced 'guyting'.

🖉 From the car park walk back to the village centre and keep ahead to cross the main street. Descend a cul-de-sac and cross a small stream. Cross a stile and follow the stream to its confluence with a greater stream (a tributary of the River Windrush).

Go over the footbridge and fork right **A** on to the footpath that enters a meadow. The beautiful Windrush valley is to the right. Cross the meadow to stiles that take it through paddocks at Little Windrush Farm. Turn left at the lane. There are good views of Guiting Wood (and the Manor House) as you pass Castlett Farm (note its fine barn). The site of an abandoned medieval village is to the right as you come to Critchford Lane.

Turn left and go down to the ford where the stream is crossed by a

> **The Wardens' Way** links Bourton-on-the-Water to Winchcombe and can be combined with the Windrush Way to make a 26-mile (42km) circular route. The Wardens' Way was created with the help of the Cotswold Voluntary Warden Service, hence its name.

PUBLIC TRANSPORT Tel. 01452 425543
REFRESHMENTS Pubs in Guiting Power (both cater for children)
PUBLIC TOILETS None
ORDNANCE SURVEY MAPS Outdoor Leisure 45 (The Cotswolds)

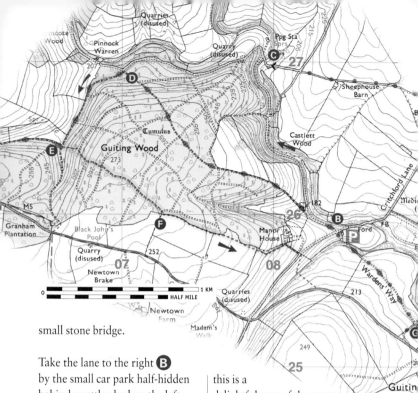

small stone bridge.

Take the lane to the right
by the small car park half-hidden
behind a cattle-shed on the left.

The lane follows the west flank of
the valley above the small stream –

> **Temple Guiting and Guiting
> Power** are neighbouring
> villages in the Windrush valley. It is
> easy to see how Temple Guiting came
> by its name – the land here belonged
> to the Knights Templar. Less easily
> explained is Guiting Power. Although it
> could have referred to the fulling mills
> that were a feature of the valley from
> Norman times onwards, in fact it
> takes the name of a local family.
> 'Guiting' is from an Old English word
> meaning a flood.

this is a
delightful part of the route.
Look out for herons fishing in
the small pond passed after
½ mile (800m). Go left at a
T-junction **C**.

A steep climb follows but the
gradient soon eases. After ¾ mile
(1.2km), where the lane bends
right and begins to descend, two
footpaths leave to the left **D**. Take
the one on the right that more or
less follows the line of the lane –
not the one that climbs directly
uphill. The path soon reaches the
western edge of the wood.

Keep along the edge of the wood to a footpath crossways **E**. Turn left on to a narrow path that climbs into trees. It is steep at first and there are wooden steps to provide good footholds in the ground that is often muddy. The path broadens when the gradient becomes easier. Keep ahead when paths cross.

When the path is close to the edge of

 What is a fulling mill?

the wood **F**, take a lesser path to the right for 50 yds (46m) (unfortunately the waymark here has been lost) to the edge of the wood and turn left on to a field edge giving vistas of miles of open country to the right. If the path has been recently used by horses it may be muddy. The path passes close to the manor-house with its unusual lantern on top of its roof. Turn right at the drive and then take the second left at the lane (not over the cattle-grid) and walk back to the small car park **B**.

Turn right just before the car park to follow the Wardens' Way sign on a track descending to a gate. After this it climbs through fields before coming to a T-junction **G**.

Turn left to descend to a stream, which the Wardens' Way follows to a lane into Guiting Power. Go left at the main road and then turn right after the war memorial to return to the village hall and the starting point.

Guiting Power

20 *Bibury and Coln St Aldwyns*

Bibury is one of the 'must see' Cotswold places, and this walk takes you to corners not seen by most visitors. The riverside walk to Coln St Aldwyns, another delightful village, is through verdant countryside that is at its best in summer – the going may be moist at other times. The return leg is mainly on a bridleway that crosses open country, most of it pastureland. The place-names may be confusing here – Bibury is on the north bank of the River Coln, Arlington on the south, while Ablington is just a mile (1.6km) upstream.

START Arlington Mill

DISTANCE 6½ miles (10.5km)

TIME 3 hours

PARKING Finding space at Bibury is difficult at peak times. There is a small car park opposite Arlington Mill, roadside parking by the river and byway parking in streets near the church

ROUTE FEATURES Some gradients and muddy ground at times; footpath may cross cultivated land

With Arlington Mill to the right, climb the main road away from the River Coln past the post office and the Catherine Wheel inn. Take the footpath on the left immediately after the pub **Ⓐ** and climb the left-hand side of a field to a gate and stone stile.

Go over the stile and keep ahead on a path that gives tantalising views of the village below. This hillside is quaintly known as Awkward Hill. A wooden gate takes the path through a stand of fine beeches. After the cricket pavilion bear right to the corner of the field where there is a stile. The path goes along the edge of a wood to another stile.

PUBLIC TRANSPORT Tel. 01452 425543

REFRESHMENTS Tearoom at Arlington Mill, pubs at Bibury and Coln St Aldwyns

PUBLIC TOILETS On Bibury main street

ORDNANCE SURVEY MAPS Outdoor Leisure 45 (The Cotswolds)

Which well-known cleric is connected with Coln St Aldwyns?

Continue to follow the wall on the right, cross a third, high stile and join a bridleway where it comes to the top of a rise. Follow the bridleway along the side of the valley – it becomes narrow as it drops down to a gate, stone stile, and footbridge **B**.

Cross the meadow to a metal gate leading to a short section, which is often flooded. Walkers have made an alternative path through trees on the right. Be careful not to tread on bluebells. A lovely section of riverside walking ends just before a weir. The path veers right by a shaky signpost to head towards a wood.

The path follows the edge of the wood and Coln St Aldwyns' larger buildings can be seen ahead. A gate, bearing a notice warning of

The stone-roofed cottages of **Arlington Row** probably date from the late 14th century when they were built as sheephouses. When weaving became important about 200 years later they were converted into cottages. Henry Ford wished to export them to the United States in the 1920s but they were saved by the intervention of the Gloucestershire Archaeological Trust and are now in the care of the National Trust.

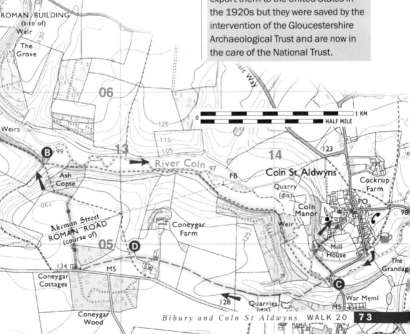

Bibury and Coln St Aldwyns WALK 20 **73**

adders, leads into a beautiful meadow. The footpath ends at Yew Tree Lodge **C**.

Turn left, cross the river and turn left on to a driveway going to Mill House. Turn right before the mill to cross the race on to a narrow footpath that climbs to a lane. The church is a few steps to the left but the route continues ahead to pass pensioners' cottages built from the stone and timber from the demolished Victorian

Bibury was acclaimed by William Morris as the most beautiful village in England and thousands of tourists spend moments here each year before dashing off to new beauty spots. The walker who lingers here will discover a lovely church with Saxon details, a famous inn, picturesque mills, and quiet corners like The Square occupied by delightful cottages. There is also Bibury Court, a Tudor building enlarged by Sir Thomas Sackville in 1633 and now a hotel.

wings of Williamstrip House in 1947.

At the crossroads by the post office at the centre of the village, turn right down the road to Quenington and pass the New Inn on the left. The road accompanies the river back to the bridge. Cross it and turn right to pass Yew Tree Lodge again **C**. Go through the gate and keep ahead on a bridle-way, climbing past ash and beech trees.

The River Coln and Bibury Court

After a stretch of pleasant parkland walking, the bridleway crosses a large and then a smaller field to pass cottages on the right and a barn on the left to a metal gate  **D**. Head for the house ahead at the corner of a large field and go through a gate on to the road. Walk for about 50 yds (46m) along the road before turning right on a farm track running between two houses and heading towards woods.

Arlington Row

In spring, bluebells line the track as it crosses Akeman Street (there is no trace of the Roman road on the ground here). Turn left by the hollow oak at the top corner of Ash Copse and follow its edge to a gate at the other corner. From here you will see the footbridge crossed earlier **B**. Climb the slope after the stone stile and keep on the track for about a mile (1.6km) to pass Court Farm (the grand house on the right) and the disused water mill to the left.

There is a good view of Bibury Court to the left beyond a weir.

Turn left at the lane and left again at the main road. Leave it to the left at the telephone-box to walk past a lovely group of cottages set around The Square and continue to the school and church. Keep ahead after this down the one-way street, which follows the River Coln and joins the main road.

Cross the pretty footbridge to see Arlington Row, Bibury's world-famous group of 14th-century cottages. Turn right at the end of the row on to an asphalted footpath on the west side of the river. The water meadow to the right is the Rack Isle, where cloth dyed at Arlington Mill was dried. The footpath reaches the road opposite the Mill. ●

Further Information

Walking Safety

Although the reasonably gentle countryside that is the subject of this book offers no real dangers to walkers at any time of the year, it is still advisable to take sensible precautions and follow certain well-tried guidelines.

Always take with you both warm and waterproof clothing and sufficient food and drink. Wear suitable footwear, i.e. strong walking boots or shoes that give a good grip over stony ground, on slippery slopes and in muddy conditions. Try to obtain a local weather forecast and bear it in mind before you start. Do not be afraid to abandon your proposed route and return to your starting point in the event of a sudden and unexpected deterioration in the weather.

All the walks described in this book will be safe to do, given due care and respect, even during the winter. Indeed, a crisp, fine winter day often provides perfect walking conditions, with firm ground underfoot and a clarity unique to this time of the year.

The most difficult hazard likely to be encountered is mud, especially

The Mill at Lower Slaughter

when walking along woodland and field paths, farm tracks and bridleways – the latter in particular can often get churned up by cyclists and horses. In summer, an additional difficulty may be narrow and over-grown paths, particularly along the edges of cultivated fields. Neither should constitute a major problem provided that the appropriate footwear is worn.

Hailes Abbey

Follow the Country Code

- Enjoy the countryside and respect its life and work
- Guard against all risk of fire
- Take your litter home
- Fasten all gates
- Help to keep all water clean
- Keep your dogs under control
- Protect wildlife, plants and trees
- Keep to public paths across farmland
- Take special care on country roads
- Leave livestock, crops and machinery alone
- Make no unnecessary noise
- Use gates and stiles to cross fences, hedges and walls

    (The Countryside Agency)

The Cotswold Voluntary Warden Service

The Cotswold Voluntary Warden Service was formed in 1968 in order to assist in the preservation and promotion of the Cotswolds Area of Outstanding Natural Beauty.

The principal objectives of the Service are: to provide facilities which improve public access and enjoyment of the countryside; to promote the qualities of the countryside, thereby enhancing the public's appreciation of them; and to protect the countryside from excessive, potentially damaging use.

Misarden Park

The Service is administered by Gloucestershire County Council. Further information can be obtained from: Cotswold Warden Office, County Planning Department, Shire Hall, Gloucester GL1 2TN. Tel. 01452 452674

Useful Organisations

Council for the Protection of Rural England
Warwick House,
25 Buckingham Palace Road,
London SW1W 0PP.
Tel. 020 7976 6433

Countryside Agency
John Dower House,
Crescent Place, Cheltenham,
Gloucestershire GL50 3RA.
Tel. 01242 521381

English Heritage
23 Savile Row, London W1X 1AB.
Tel. 0171 973 3250
www.english-heritage.org.uk

Gloucestershire County Council
Environment Department
Tel. 01452 425577

English Nature
Northminster House,
Peterborough, Cambs. PE1 1UA.
Tel. 01733 455100
E-mail: enquiries@english-nature.org.uk
www.english-nature.org.uk

National Trust
Membership and general enquiries:
PO Box 39, Bromley,
Kent BR1 3XL.
Tel. 0181 315 1111

E-mail: enquires@ntrust.org.uk
Regional offices:
Gloucestershire: Mythe End House,
Tewkesbury, Glos. GL20 6EB.
Tel. 01684 850051
Oxfordshire: Hughenden Manor,
High Wycombe, Bucks. HP14 4LA.
Tel. 01494 528051

Ordnance Survey
Romsey Road, Maybush,
Southampton SO16 4GU.
Tel. 08456 05 05 05 (Lo-call)

Oxfordshire County Council
Countryside Service
Tel. 01865 810226

Ramblers' Association
2nd Floor, Camelford House,
87–90 Albert Embankment,
London SE1 7TW.
Tel. 020 7339 8500

Heart of England Tourist Board
Woodside, Larkhill Road,
Worcester WR5 2EF.
Tel. 01905 763436
Fax 01905 763450
*Local tourist information centres
(*not open all year):*
Abingdon: 01235 522711
Bourton-on-the-Water: 01451 820211
Burford: 01993 823558
Cheltenham Spa: 01242 522878
Chipping Norton: 01608 644379
Cirencester: 01285 654180

Coleford: 01594 812388
Gloucester: 01452 421188
Newent: 01531 822468
*Northleach: 01451 860715
Stow-on-the-Wold: 01451 831082
Stroud: 01453 765768
Tetbury: 01666 503552
Tewkesbury: 01684 295027
*Winchcombe: 01242 602925
Witney: 01993 775802
Woodstock: 01993 775802

Youth Hostels Association
Trevelyan House,
8 St Stephen's Hill,
St Albans, Herts. AL1 2DY.
Tel. 01727 855215 (gen. enquiries)
Tel. 01727 845047
E-mail: customerservices@yha.org.uk
Travel line: 0870 608 2608

*Ordnance Survey Maps
of the Cotswolds*
Outdoor Leisure map 45 (The
Cotswolds), Explorer maps 168
(Stroud, Tetbury & Malmsbury)
and 179 (Gloucester, Cheltenham
& Stroud), Landranger 163
(Cheltenham & Cirencester)

Answers to Questions
Walk 1: Workmen would collect
ice from lakes and ponds during
the winter and it would be stored
underground in the ice-house.
Walk 2: The 132ft- (40m) high
tower, built in 1400, was funded by

the properties of the earls of Kent and Salisbury, who rebelled against Henry IV but were captured and beheaded by citizens.

Walk 3: On the estate cottages opposite the Victoria Inn.

Walk 4: The distinctive scratches show that badgers often clamber over this stone stile.

Walk 5: To a water deity.

Walk 6: Many famous jockeys used to trained on Cleeve Common, among them Fred Archer, whose ghost is supposed to haunt Prestbury.

Walk 7: Thirteen people!

Walk 8: The fearsome gargoyles on St Laurence's Church.

Walk 9: Edward Thomas made Adlestrop famous by describing an unscheduled halt when he was on his way to visit his friend and fellow poet Robert Frost.

> Yes I remember Adlestrop –
> The name, because one afternoon
> Of heat the express train drew up there
> Unwontedly. It was late June.
>
> The steam hissed. Someone cleared his throat.
> No one left and no one came
> On the bare platform. What I saw
> Was Adlestrop – only the name.

Subsequently Thomas was killed in France on 9 April 1917.

Walk 10: Cliff Well carries the inscription:

> Go seek that well which never faileth.

Walk 11: Holy Trinity Church reflects the Minchinhampton's importance in the wool trade.

Walk 12: Littleworth Wood is coppiced woodland. The slender growth of ash is now used for fencing or thatching but was previously made into broomsticks.

Walk 13: At the height of its prosperity in the 1880s Blockley's silk mills supplied Coventry's ribbon-makers, so when fashion changed and that industry failed, Blockley's fortune also suffered.

Walk 14: A monument in St John the Baptist's Church to Edmund Harman, who was Henry VIII's barber, has Red Indians dancing around the lettering!

Walk 15: There is a delightful carving in the porch of the Church of Sts Peter and Paul of a cat playing a fiddle to three rats.

Walk 16: Viollet-le-Duc deplored the use of wood or metal in Gothic revival buildings.

Walk 17: The Roman 2nd Legion – no doubt with many British slaves.

Walk 18: A mischievous or evil spirit, immortalised in Shakespeare's *Midsummer Night's Dream*.

Walk 19: A mill where fuller's earth was used to make permanent the colours dyed into cloth.

Walk 20: The father of John Keble (1792–1866), Anglican churchman and poet, was vicar at Coln St Aldwyns for fifty-three years from 1782, his son serving as curate for ten years until 1835.